Reaching for the Dawn

Christine E Power

:

...and the woman exhales with a deep sigh of release and the sound is a whisper in the lightest winds through a massive canyon - barely heard yet harshly felt. It is coming - am I ready?

CONTENTS- CHAPTERS

Forward

My life has not been unique; many people have survived child sexual abuse - that is something I had to learn - I thought I was alone. What may differ from person to person is the degree to which these experiences affect and shape the adult we become. It is important for me to write about it because writing allows me to purge the past and set those experiences free so they don't cause emotional turmoil now. I am coming to terms with my past and beginning to hope for an astounding future.

There were times when I was so confused and deeply depressed that suicide seemed the only way to get relief; however, I rejected it each time because of the extreme hurt it would cause to family and friends and the legacy my name would permanently carry. These were enough to make me pause.

Before I began therapy, the things that enabled me to survive were: disappearing (dissociating), mentally shutting down, denial, fantasy, changing my behavior and/or my appearance, memory repression, etc. These were not effective in keeping me healthy.

At first, I thought therapy was an invasion of my privacy. Revealing my secrets to someone I barely knew did not appeal to me. Especially, since I was ashamed and sure that everything about the abuse was my fault.

Part of the problem was that I did not know what I really wanted and I did not think it was important or possible to allow myself to be happy. So, I decided therapy was not an option for me. Instead I endeavored to "fix" myself, privately, with self-help books. They did very little to help, just made everything more confusing, and seemed to be saying that what happened was not a big deal and suggested "skills" to help me "get over it".

Finally, when despite all my efforts, I was still depressed and suicidal, I asked for help from a therapist. Surprised that I actually trusted another human being with my past, I began talking. I learned life skills and coping skills, and learned to journal. I was diagnosed with Bipolar Disorder II and began taking medications for it. My mood stabilized and my life began to turn around.

My days have not always been filled with sadness, fear, anxiety, depression, and feeling out-of-control; there have been times when I felt comfortable in this world and genuinely happy. There have been countless times when I laughed so hard that I cried. These are memories I hold close to my heart.

Change did not come easy for me. It took a while for me to figure out that if I wanted things to get better, I had to work hard to make it happen - not wait for it to happen on its own. Eventually, I learned that it is possible and desirable to make healthy choices for myself instead of letting myself slowly die.

Now, laughter and happiness is everything to me and it feels so sweet.

CHAPTER 1 - FROM DREAMS

Creatures From Under the Stairs

See snakes slither in your moonlit kitchen.
As they invade your beautiful home,
A thick, freezing mist fills the midnight air.
Evil inhabits this house below the stairs.

Frightened, you awaken from a restless sleep.
Something is wrong and the feeling runs deep.
As you reflect on events from another day,
Something moves in the darkened hall way.

Countless pairs of red glowing eyes-
Sit and watch you like so many spies.
Then small ugly creatures leap from the shadows-
Start biting your legs and reaching for elbows.

You run like mad as they come close behind-squealing.
Blood splatters clothes, the walls, carpets, and ceiling.
Reaching your bedroom, you slam the door screaming.
You lock the door and pray that you've escaped -
kneeling.

But wood is a snack for these foul, angry monsters.
They claw and chew and shred the temporary gate.
As the last of the door splinters and falls to the floor,
A way out occurs to you when you can't endure more.

Taking a deep breath and closing your eyes,
You let out a scream so loud it surprised,
"I'm sorry, please forgive me my sweet demon child".

5

Christine E Power

The creature's face softened like dough, then she cried.

She surveyed my wounds - all was set right and healed.
The entry to the stairs was packed tight and sealed.
Finally, the nightmare dissolves and flows away-
a river of red and black images from the fray.

Exhausted and alone in your beautiful home -
just the sound of a clock ticking in the next room.
Sitting in your rocking chair with a blanket and hot coffee.
Comfort sweet comfort with a piece of rich toffee.

The sun is rising, signaling the start of a bright new day.
And you know sleep will not come easy for a while.
Then you hear a faint creak under the stairs.

Cyber Leprosy

I carry the grotesque sores of Cyber Leprosy. The electronic rivers of information and communication flow away, not towards me. My questions and inquiries might be answered, but only after long silences. Are they afraid of catching some foul electronic disease from me? My turn will come for answers. Meanwhile, I am an idea floating through space that is nothing until it finds a home in a human mind and expands.

I feel this isolation like a vast desert continent of hot, blinding white sand; which when blown in a fierce wind, scratches my face raw and gets into my eyes. When someone finally comes to answer my question, I have forgotten the question. Will my memory become like an endless library but there is no key to the door? No password to access my files? Will my memories, that are my identity, be destroyed or become inaccessible or obsolete?

As I start to recognize my failures and impending mental and physical decline, my breathing becomes heavy and strained, panic sets in, and tears roll down my face as I cry silently. My throat squeezes down and I cannot speak. Others' tension, anger, and annoyance are basted over me like extra spicy BBQ sauce. Am I to be grilled or dismissed or both?

Silence again. I am a Cyber Leper - distanced from people who would rather not communicate with me, in any form, for fear that what I have is contagious.

So, I sit here and pick my sores and hum favorite songs of long ago. Then I hear a siren approaching - "ah, my ride is here". Nice men stand in front of me and say, "Come with us; we will take you to a place that's happy and bright." As they take me away, I try to show them my sores, but they are gone now.

And when that final bit of electronic data calls but misses me, I have already gone willingly.

And the black crow gladly takes my sand-filled eyes.

The Dream Demons

As I continue my determined march thru life, nightmares still rob my soul of complete peace.

Dream demons rip at my torn sleeves or whatever clothing they can grab. They scratch my skin with sharp claws and I can feel warm blood soaking through my blouse and dripping down my arms and hands. They are more silent than a whisper, but fiercely angry and violent as they chase me through my nightmares.

In desperate fear, I increase my pace to a sprint, gasping for each faint breath. With steamy sweat dripping from my nose, I try to escape. But they are still there, I can sense it, as if they are riding my straining back up each steep hill and around every sharp corner.

They stare at me with red, hot glowing eyes that burn images of torture into my present conscience mind.

Other people in these dreams look frozen as statues, unable or afraid to help.

I have conquered these dream warriors many times.
Why do they return to challenge me?
To destroy me and drag me into their cold dark world where I would be like them - lost mind, body, and soul?

The Royal Blue Satin Gown

A talented old seamstress recalls a pattern left aside, but not forgotten. She pulls on the brass knobs to a thick, heavy drawer. There jammed in the back is the delicate, yellowed tissue of a pattern for illness - a royal blue satin, exquisite burial gown to be made for a woman who lived with stress, oppression, depression, and madness. In the fog of mental weakness, she decided how and when she would die - if for no other reason, than to have control over it. Toward this end, she commissioned a fancy new dress for the occasion.

The tailor spread the thin, transparent pattern across an antique mahogany work table. Her hands tremble from memory and the pain of arthritis. Then she turned, with the agility and speed of youth, bounced around the tiny shop gathering fabric, thread, beads, lace, chains, crystals, braided rope, lining, and other adornments. She worked without thought, like walking down a familiar path for the thousandth time. But, as pieces of the dress came together and started to take form, she realized now as she did before - it is not her time to go.

Her glasses fell off as she dropped her head to the work table, and her hands slid safely away from the unfinished cloth and gown. She gently refolded the yellowed delicate pattern and quietly returned it to the thick heavy drawer with the brass knobs at the back of the store. A gown, perhaps, never to be created.

The Hawk

As the powerful hawk circles gracefully above,
Waiting for a moment of weakness - I quiver.
In the vast barren desert, I see not the hawk's tail,
But talons, beak, and focused eyes.
It descends to cross my unbroken path.
Does he seek me as his prey?
To rip and devour until I am a
White, shining skeleton in the burning desert sun?

Dancing With the Devil

Let the sun cool down your heaving breasts-
And a soldier's hands to heal the rest.
Beautiful, soothing music takes you to the next level.
Dance while you play with, then reject the devil.
To feel more alive, you must BE more alive.
Dip in the cold, teal blue waters;
and emerge clean and wise-
Knowing what really matters.

Let Go of Your Panic

Pause and let go of your panic.
Breathe deeply.
Allow your nightmares to slip back where they came rom.
Reach out to touch a bright star in the dark night sky.
Watch it shoot away as if it were startled, leaving behind a long tail of shiny, silver dust, and sparkling light.
The star has left behind a special gift for you-
    a dream filled with everything and everyone you treasure, that which excites you, stimulates your imagination, and teases all of your senses.
So lose yourself in a dream world of fantasy
and return refreshed and strong.

Slaying a Sly Demon – Medieval Style

Come hither sly demon lest I slay you with sharpened speech.
I'll clench violently with crooked ends, places others dare not reach.

I fear not your rage and fiery complexion.
Your lies and deceit make me desire truth and reflection.

Though merciless torture feeds your blackened heart,
I stand unafraid - I've seen the worst of your bloody art.

I hath fury of my own - a tornado of power and light.
I've grown teeth sharp like razors and superhuman might.

Growing accustomed to darkness, I no longer fear the night.
I smell your sour stench – like a coward, you hide out of sight.

So come hither sly demon - there's a wild chill in the air.
To wait any longer would be too much to bare.

For now, I am feeling courageous and strong.
Killing this menacing devil - I've had the advantage all along.

Where Love Has Time for Me

I love you past ten pm,
When I live behind my eyes.
Where birds swim, fish fly, and rivers run uphill.
Hours last for a minute and minutes last for a day.

Smiling, you appear from out of the mist.
With you, I feel safe and confident.
Your expressions are comforting and gratuitous.
Your arms are strong, warm, yielding and tender.

Glowing eyes foretell your desire.
Proud shyness sheds its timid skin
    As I stroke your liquid body.
Our souls, transparent, gather each other.
Then ecstasy sighs with unheard cries -
    A frictionless sensual climax.

By daylight you have vanished.
My arms feel vacant and melancholy.
No longer performing miraculous stunts,
I plunge through my day alone.
No time for romance until evening again.

When I love you past ten pm
And I live behind my eyes
Where love has time for me.

A Dream of My Son

Tonight I had a powerful dream, one that seemed to last the entire night - I dreamed of my life with my son.

It begins with me free falling in the pitch dark and screaming. At this point, I was aware that I was dreaming but was curious and allowed the dream to continue.

I was in a hospital bed drenched with sweat, exhausted, and in pain. He was placed into my arms - a treasure to change my life. I was overjoyed and very scared. My son had wavy brown hair and warm brown eyes.

He looked at me with intensity and affection. He liked it when I ran my fingers through his hair as he sat on my lap and we had conversations about life and the world.

I was proud when he, borrowing a bicycle from the neighbors, taught himself how to ride a bike. He got good grades, had a few close friends, he was a thinker, and a dreamer, practical, and truly cared about other people. When he started talking about girls, I tried to give him "the talk", but he said he already knew about sex.

I saw many scenes of him reading in a lush green meadow, on a beach by the ocean, and in a park at the base of an enormous mountain.

He had a fascination with hand to hand combat video games so he chose Boxing as his activity for competition and fitness. I did not like for him to box. Many times he came home with his eyes and face puffy, bleeding, and sore. I understood that boxing is a sport of art and strategy, but it disturbed me that it was also about violence and brutality and may cause permanent damage to his beautiful face. Or worse.

He was an artist - talented with a brush, and painted bright and unusual pictures. One picture was of me with a missing eye - I'm not sure what that symbolizes (to dream that I am seeing a painting of me with a missing eye and it was painted by a son I never had – analyze that).

One day, he brought home a girl for me to meet, I liked her immediately and thought they would be happy together.

Then, one cold and snowy winter day, my son and I were driving to a friend's house in the mountains. He was driving. The roads were very icy, and people were driving too fast for the conditions. Then a large truck up ahead lost control and spun around hitting and crushing vehicles in its path. In a flash our car was caught up in the wreck. I had remained in the car, but I did not see my son right away. Miraculously, I only had some cuts and bruises, but I was not concerned with myself. Our car had been tossed in a ditch and my son had been thrown from the car. He was barely conscious and blood seemed to be streaming from him everywhere. I carefully took him in my arms and screamed "Help. Somebody Help!". He said, "It's okay mom, I will not be needing help. Then softly he said, "It has been worth it Mom. The time we spent together has been worth everything." I said, "Yes it was worth it. I love you, Son" as the life drained from his eyes and the warmth slipped from his body. Then I buried my face in his chest and cried a miserable cry so deep that it drained all my energy and took my breath away, leaving me feeling depressed, flat, and alone in the world.

He was born into my arms and died in my arms - all in one night. A miracle. His name was never revealed to me. When I woke up, it felt like something important had happened – that I had been changed in a positive way. I felt empty but blessed - then I began to recall this dream and write what I could remember. I am glad to have had this experience of life and love- if only in a night long dream of my son.

Kept Safe By a Lion

A large proud, male lion comes to my front door every day. He climbs the cement steps, turns to face the road, and lays with his strong paws extended forward. His brilliant, honey colored main shines in the sunlight and feathers in the warm breeze. His dark round eyes are focused and alert. His movements are relaxed, slow, and deliberate.

He is here for me.

He is the guardian of my wellness, safety, and my soul.

He gives me strength to stand out in the world and
    roar for what is right.

He gives me the hunger I need to take huge bites of the
    good things in life.

He gives me courage to keep moving forward during the
    hard times.

He reminds me to appreciate how lucky I have been,
    the lessons I have learned, and the love I have
    shared.

Knowing generosity feeds my soul, he has seen the
    good that I have done for people.

When my day is done, I sit quietly with this mighty lion on the front steps and brush my hand along his curved back. He turns and looks me in the eye as if to say he approves. He is more like a large, purring cat than a fierce wild animal- I am safe with him and I do not fear him. And, as the sun begins to set in a brilliant orange sky, my lion steps into the night with his tail swaying gracefully from side to side. He turns to give me one last glance, then steps into my dreams to keep my soul safe there too.

Message In a Dream

I was having another night of insomnia, so I decided to see if a walk would help. Down a dark sidewalk in the middle of the night, there was someone sitting awkwardly against a cold, brick building almost invisible in the glow of the street light. A thin, almost skeletal, hand reached out as if urging me to stop. As I stepped closer, I could see that it was an old woman. Her eyes were black and blue spiral pools without true focus. Yet, in her blindness, she could see my shame as if we were connected and familiar. I could sense her profound wisdom through her physical poverty. She was barely covered in black shredded clothes that offered no comfort against the chilly night and she sat shaking uncontrollably trying to wrap strips of cloth around her like a shawl. My heart ached for her and I wondered what brought her to such a tortured state. I offered to bring her a coat, a blanket, and some hot food, but she refused. I began to think she was a ghost or a dream, there to impart an important message to me.

Then she spoke in loud, powerful thoughts. "Allow the difficult times in life to shape your compassion and empathy toward others. Don't let sorrow build a home of mistrust and bitterness in your heart. Satisfaction in helping others in need will strengthen your lust for life. So when the hard times come, you will remember that things were and can be better. This you have already learned, but hold it close for natural ups and downs are at the core of living and make it rich and complete."

After imparting her message, the woman completely disappeared. I was walking again as if it never happened.

Walking and getting nowhere. Then it occurred to me that I was actually asleep and dreaming. I woke up with the woman's words playing in my mind- her message was part of my life philosophy already, but it does not hurt to be reminded.

Your life is enriched by helping others.

Rise Great Phoenix

After a cruel demon's flames have scorched the land and sky, shake off the dirt and grime.

Spread your broad, injured wings great Phoenix.

Rise from the hot, steamy embers and gray, powdery ashes.

Take flight to a peaceful blue-green sea where waves slide along sandy beaches under refreshing, cool breezes.

Your body will be warmed and healed by the sun, and your feathers can rest softly in the sand and shine.

When revived and strong, and only then,
return to avenge the horror and take a foul demon to a black flaming hell of its own.

On the Wings of a Cool Night Breeze

A soft breeze whispers through the crisp night air.
It holds the blue, liquid secrets to my life's despair.
It calls to me with a voice that's sad and mellow,
in a shy whistle through my open window.

Embracing this whispering wind, I observe it with interest.
I hold it safe and still against my shivering chest.
Then I listen to this voice carefully to understand
that which has made me who I am.

I am proud for what I was able to survive
and what I have accomplished in my life.
It cannot be taken all at once; too much intensity,
too much history, too much struggle;
but a lot of laughter, and hope too.

So I set it free to disappear on the wings of the cool night
breeze, knowing it will fly back to me again- some night.
When the winds are gentle, and cool, and whispering.

Christine E Power

In the Blackness of Night

The blackness of night -
a dark star's time to shine.
Comets are ideas in flight.

A whisper at midnight is truth finally spoken.
The stars hold safe the records and secrets of time.
Sadness lives in the coolness of the shadows.
Fear and horror lurk among the lifeless trees.

And a journey thru your dreams tonight could mean
ecstasy with the stars as you fly thru the night
leaving a trail of beautiful light behind.

Butterfly Dancing in the Mountain Rain

She glides quietly, secretly, by the light of the moon in flowing purples and blues - dancing.

And dreams incredible fantasies filled with vibrant color, powerful emotions, and intensified senses.

In day light, she spreads her soft, colorful wings and moves, with ease, to the rhythms of life.

And when rain falls, she bravely turns into it instead of away - flying higher, meeting the challenge - not diving.

Proving she is strong enough to fly to the top of a mountain with the weight of rain on her wings, alone.

Her resilience and strength are impressive and give courage to the rest of us to find wings of our own.

A survivor as such, she still brings comfort to others - and is a beautiful soul to behold as she flies away with grace - again.

My Intuition About What My Soul Is

I believe the soul is a great information gatherer - it knows every thought, experience, and dream I ever had. It stores all things I have seen, heard, touched, felt, tasted, hated and loved. It knows the emotional and physical pain I have experienced and how I dealt with it. It knows my opinions, beliefs, and aspirations. My soul knows what makes me happy and lifts me high with joy. It knows the absolute truth- always.

The soul cannot be injured or destroyed, but it's luster and light can become dim; it can lose inspiration and the lust for life. I need to feed my soul by doing nice things for others. It helps counter the negativity I've experienced in my lifetime, brings balance, and gives my soul positive strength. Doing this may also bring me closer to learning what my soul was meant to learn in this lifetime (although it could be something negative) - allowing this life to end in a natural way. Too much negativity makes the soul sick and diminishes its strength to the point of no longer gathering information. Then the lesson that is supposed to be learned may be missed, prolonging life in the physical body. With positive energy, personal growth, love, and learning the light in my soul becomes brighter and the peace I feel inside is relaxing and warm. I become more brave, confident, and comfortable.

Since my soul holds so much knowledge about me, it is an excellent source to help me make important decisions about my present and future. The hard part is to access this information - soul searching.

The soul is where mysterious talents come from-
intuition, ESP, the ability to see far into the past and
future. I believe I have a strong intuition. Many people
have told me that I seem to be an "old soul"- not
necessarily one who has many past lives (nor famous
ones), but one who has gathered great knowledge from
these past lives. Even as a small child, I seemed mature
and thought deeply and asked important questions.

In times of extreme fear, extreme danger, and extreme
emotional and physical pain, my soul has rescued me by
pulling the awareness out of my body. I would be on the
ceiling looking down like a light fixture. I had no feeling in
my body, no sense of my heartbeat; the panic, fear, and
pain were gone. I was just watching from above. I
thought this was what it must be like to be a ghost. This
did not last long - I was returned to my body when the
worst was over. My soul helped me in this way so I could
survive the experience without losing my sanity forever. I
later described this phenomenon to my therapists as
disappearing.

My mother believed that our souls were put on earth to
learn something (which is never revealed to us); and
once we have learned that something, we can die and our
souls are free to move on. A soul does not die - it adds its
knowledge to the universe - and with the slate wiped
clean (or at least nearly so), begins a new life in a new
body or simply becomes part of the universe.

When I die, my soul will be free to soar through the sky
and touch huge white clouds - to ride the brisk wind, to
be the rain, and sit inside electric lightning - to see every
majestic mountaintop, powerful waterfall, and calming

stream and to swim each stormy sea. I will discover what it feels like to be a towering maple tree, a Hummingbird, a red Rose, an intelligent dolphin, and a wild bee. I will spend a day on the wings of a large blue dragonfly. At sunrise, I will sit in a lush, green meadow covered in mist and the cool morning dew; and listen to plants and flowers reach for the sun. I will linger for a moment in the mind of a proud African Lioness. I will see all the wonders of the world and a hundred days worth of sunrises and sunsets. I will visit the living I left behind, hug their hearts, and leave a message of love and hope. Then, when the colored maple leaves and rose petals scatter, I will exit the Earth to travel through the universe where I will embrace the souls that came before me. Now-these things only happen in dreams- but when I die and my soul is free, the things I can do and learn are limitless.

My soul is where I feel things most deeply and it will be with me always, so I will continue to do things that will feed or enhance my soul until it is a beautiful, rainbow colored, light in the distant universe.

CHAPTER 2 - TIMES OF STRUGGLE

Get Away!

Get away!
You make my skin crawl.
You like to bite me:
I wish you would not.
You try to get in my pants:
Can't you behave yourself?
You want my food -
you want my blood?
Well, you can't have them!
So, there!
I brush you off:
You always return.
You like to get on my nerves
Don't you, you little bug.

And I Shiver

My heart beat is pounding in my chest and ears. Fear wraps around me like a thin blanket in the cold. It is silent in the faint pre-dawn light of my room.
And I shiver.

Soon the nightmares and room invaders will melt into the walls.

Light creeps along the walls, ceiling, and hard wood floors until my room is bathed with a bleaching sunlight - harsh and oppressive - not pleasant as most say it is.

I stare at my reflection in the mirror in the bathroom. This is when I rebuild myself in preparation for the day. Trying to change the image I see - smiles and strength are a tightly fitted mask. No one will ask then, no one will ask. It is another life for me in the daylight hours. I leave the house in a natural disguise.

The day consists of many interactions with people known and unknown - for business and casual conversation. Laughing and smiling are good camouflage - no one notices, asks, or cares that I am slowly dying inside. I prefer that they are all left unaware. I am lost in a sea of people, all the same.

My work, at least, provides suitable distraction and I am able to forget for a while.

I'm told forgiveness is for me - for my peace of mind, for my "letting go", and the ones I forgive may never know.

Yet I still clench tightly my anger to my chest.

As night time approaches, and the sun sets unnoticed by me, I begin the nightly compulsive ritual of collecting my anxiety, panic, and fears. Especially, fears that the past will find me in my sleep and I will be a defenseless child - unable to run, unable to scream, unable to tell...

Yes, I am an adult in complete control and not in any danger now. But still, when I awaken from these dreams, the power and intensity of the experience makes me wonder how I made it.

And I shiver.

A Brave Little Secret Keeper

I can see her, in a pink flower nightgown, alone in the dark sobbing quietly on the hardwood floor, soaking the area rug there with her tears.

Crying so deeply that it robs her of her breath and she begins to heave, trying to catch some air without making much noise.

Talking would be impossible now because her throat is squeezed tightly shut.

It feels like this monsoon will never end; and she will choke to death from the torrent of emotion.

I can see her, this shadow of myself; a brave little secret keeper, wanting someone to say it was okay – that she was okay.

But the tears MUST stop because Dad is afraid someone will ask what is wrong – and I stop crying – afraid I might tell them.

When I Lost the Ability to Cry

Somewhere between a melancholy sigh and a simple tear, my mind and body block the creation of a solitary tear – even when healthy, healing crying is something I crave.

It began when I was a 4 year old child. I realized a few things: 1) My father would punish me in a painful way if I cried. 2) He got more angry if I was crying because of something he did. 3) I would get spanked more if I continued to cry. This anger, yelling, and spanking gave my father power over me - making me feel scared and small. If I did not allow myself to cry, my painful encounters with my father over crying were eliminated.

The actual change happened one afternoon, when I was sobbing loud and hard on my bed because I had torn open my hands on the chains of the swing - I was jumping off and grabbed the chains. My hands were ripped and bleeding. My mother had tried to give first aid to me but my father, furious that I had hurt myself doing something I was told not to do, grabbed me, marched me to my room, and said that is where I would stay until morning. I cried and softly protested to myself. He was yelling from another room that he would spank me if I didn't stop crying. I got very quiet and stared at the ceiling light which was a blur through my wet swollen eyes. I swore that I would not shed another tear. Of course I do cry, rarely, but I am afraid that the tears will come in a messy flood, I will lose control, and will not be able to stop crying.

How I Forgot

This child's mind, instead of being filled with young fantasies and play, is filled with fear – few thoughts of survival or escape, but many thoughts about what it means to keep a terrible secret or die – painful, shameful, unreal, and her fault. Adult-child fantasies that were his to act out. Endlessly, she stares out windows; staring at anything and seeing nothing. It is a trance state that allows her to stay calm and not let anyone know or suspect that she holds such a strong, strange secret. She imagines what might happen if she told her teacher. Dad said, if she told anyone: her mother would not love her anymore, it would break up the family, the whole family would die, nobody would believe her, it was her fault and she would be blamed, he would not be punished and it would not stop him. He also said that this is how other fathers and daughters showed love – that it was normal and why should it bother me.

Feeling raw and defeated:
I lay on my side on the floor, curling my knees into my chest and wrapping my arms around my head, trying to block out the light, all sensations, and becoming as small as possible – thinking the smaller I am, the smaller the pain - until there is no room for the pain. But also no room for movement, speaking, hearing, memory, being... If I continue to get smaller, maybe I will completely disappear. Maybe I never was or will be.

When I found out we were moving to another city far away - something snapped in me. I went running around throwing away my dresses and skirts - mom went running behind me trying to retrieve them. She was screaming

"Stop, why are you doing this?" I didn't say anything - just kept running around looking for my skirts and dresses. TOO EASY ACCESS - I was saying no more, without actually saying it. I also demanded that my hair be cut short so I could go swimming without a bathing cap. My father was silently taking notice and believed I may tell our secret at any moment. I have no recollection of this. My mother told me about it years later. After we moved, my father left me alone (and soon started with my sister).

When it suddenly stopped, I forgot about this life with abuse, I forgot the midnight trips down the hall, I forgot the touching, whispering, pushing, embarrassment, and pain – the internal panic, the nights when tears quietly soaked my pillow until morning. I forgot that brave little soul at the edge, where sanity steals your memory so you can survive another day.

The Worst Kind of Sin

The rape of a child is the worst kind of sin.
For her to survive is a miracle.
It is sad that it's not so rare a thing
For a man to tear into soft new skin
For pleasure and power in the name of love
He takes what is not his to take.
And never considers the damage done
To the little one who must go on
In spite of the pain and the shame
And the dirty secret they share alone.
Whether she survives or not
Depends on her will to live
And her understanding that what happened
Was not her fault, not even close.

Reverberations

Blood from the genital area, scratches, soreness without
rashes,
Bruises, and bite marks; childhood innocence burned to
ashes.
In the study with the red couch and the green bankers
light,
I was forced to perform adult sex acts in the darkness of
night.

I was a worthless child - just my father's new possession.
I would run away, but my sister might suffer his affection.
The situation was hopeless; there was no help for me.
So going numb, I endured it, and buried it
subconsciously.

Throughout my entire life, I felt reverberations of the
abuse.
Shyness, shame, withdrawal, mistrust, and fear are what
I knew.
It shaped the way I related to others; it caused me to be
suspicious.
It left me with painful memories; I wished they were
fictitious.

I isolated from people even though I needed   help.
Shame became self-hatred; I wanted to kill myself.
Finally seeking help, I worked hard to make things right.
Much later, I cared about myself and more about my life.

Making a Mess of My Feelings

Making a mess of my feelings again:
Spread across the counter
And dumped on the floor
It's hard to make sense of it all

Crepe paper dreams fall apart in the breeze
Shredded pieces of memories invade
Making the present seem tainted and foul
Not anything or anyone can make me feel better.

Then: I just live there amongst the mess
I leave it, let it be what it is - accept it.
When the storm has passed, cleanup is
possible And I will start all over again.

Dread and Sadness

I am filled with dread and sadness - staring out in the distance, watching my lost soul floating around and spinning like a dust devil of smoky mist. My awareness is not aware. My senses forgot about flavor and variety. I only move when it is necessary. Showers seem pointless, but I take them for others.

That Old Blank Sadness

That old blank sadness pulls me down into the blackness
again.
White light in darkness shines through my wet, fluttering
lashes.

Past images seem in the present and dangerous behind
my eyes.
Not much to do but let it ride; part of survival and
acceptance.

The murder of a childhood is a cheap disaster-
No one notices or cares.
Yet an experienced child is wiser; called an "Old Soul".
I wear that badge of courage proudly. What else can I
do?

With the sadness and feelings of danger - still it is life on
the brink.
Still.

The Voice

The voice is a caller demanding and mean.
It insults me and commands that I leave the scene.
It sounds like a munchkin from the Wizard of Oz.
A low, growling angry voice that seems very odd.

Sometimes it screams; most times it whispers low
Behind my right ear, but it doesn't exist I know.
Medication reduces the tone and frequency I hear it.
But I still panic when it starts yelling in a fit.

Talking back to it just makes it worse.
Playing loud music makes it sing to the verse.
Ignoring it makes it mad and repeat.
Sometimes I listen in sadness and defeat.

It used to calm down when I set out to hurt myself.
Sometimes I get used to it and can ignore it without help.
Other times it is strong, repeating and insistent.
It insults me and commands me when I'm not resistant.

The last couple of years it has subsided a lot.
With work on my memories and medication I forgot
What it's like to be constantly bombarded with foul
language.
Now demands that I kill myself don't fill me with anguish.

The Fortuneteller

I'm finished with flashbacks and the mean caller.
Is it just wishful thinking;
Am I just a hopeful fortuneteller?
I won't know they're gone until I survive a past time
crawler.

I've also said I am through with suicidal oppression.
Is it just wishful thinking;
Am I just a hopeful fortuneteller?
Or is it just a matter of time before another major
depression?

With the passing of my father,
gone is my childhood offender.
Gone should be terrors related to him and all
will become mended.

Is it just wishful thinking;
Am I just a hopeful fortuneteller?
Happiness, involvement in life, and reduced fear
are what's at stake-
I can see that over the horizon -
even without a sixth sense.

What's Around the Corner?

Teary-eyed, bleary-eyed, tired and emotional,
Day after day passes by without enough rest.
Moments of clarity are prized and occasional
I can't work effectively falling asleep at my desk

Negative things said to me roll around in my mind.
Mistakes I make I magnify and obsess over.
Moments of hope and inspiration are hard to find.
I worry a depression is about to take over.

Relief from stress is found in a pack of cigarettes.
Finding time for exercise and eating right is a joke.
Looking for "him" only makes me upset.
No one wants a fat, unattractive, slob that smokes.

I'm so afraid. I am not sure what of.
What's around the corner for me if I give up?

Held Together by a Pill

I was falling apart, falling down, edgy, and sleepless.
Afraid of my intense anger, impatience, and frustration.
Trying to find a way but getting lost in my mind.
Then this pill was prescribed which slowed me down,
allowed me to sleep,
Made me mellow and at peace.
When I miss a dose of this medication, the scary
symptoms return quickly.
I feel like I am being held together by a tiny little pill.

Let That Which Burns Painfully Be Still

Don't walk carelessly into those raging flames.
Retreat slowly - respectfully.

Let that which burns painfully be still and benign.

Recall the long entrapment of your frightened, tender
soul.

Don't allow persistent visions and voices to steal joy from
the present.

The intrusive thoughts that imprison you originate
distantly.

Their timing is out of time - echoes of gripping intensity
and heat.

Strive urgently for clarity - make your weak mind
resistant.

There was no equal justice or accountability for those
crimes-

Only a supreme effort to move on despite being very
hesitant.

It is finally over - I will stand up and go on.

But the direction of my life has been altered forever.

I Choose to See What I Must See

Now I choose to see what I must see - and face what I must face- so I may understand my struggles and overcome them.

I am strong enough to make the right decisions and choices based on facts and my needs in the present moment.

I have learned that all people have some good in them, but with selfishness, greed, meanness, dishonesty, feelings of entitlement, and violence, seeing this goodness may require a powerful lens.

But it is my desire to search for this small slice of goodness - because, for me, there is a raw sweetness to life when I can humanize the wicked man even as he comes to take me away.

Mom Takes Me To The Hospital

In a dark, freezing, noise polluted hospital room, you bent and touched your soft lips to my hot frowning brow, only that one time – ever. I am sure you sensed the electric chaos that ran thru my tortured mind.

Eager pain and illness pushed forward in my body, demanding attention, triggered by nothing - unexplained - never spoken of - never attended to. Panic and darkness fogged my thinking and perception, robbing me of clear focus and the ability to remember what I loved in the world.

It seemed to me that truth was far from discovery and understanding. Touching the sharp, burning past can only hurt you if you let it. She said, "Remember, you don't always have to tell someone what you recall and how you have been hurt- it makes abuse real in the present." No Mom, the damage is already real in the present. It is too late to forget, too late to minimize, too late to hold back, too late for denial, too late to keep secrets anymore, and too late to edit what I say to people about it.

Instead, Mom, I am in need of an exorcism or a eulogy.

The Singer

In July of 1997, it was extremely hot in the City. I had been admitted into a psychiatric hospital for depression and suicidal thinking and planning - what else? The ward was located in a high rise building next to a Park. The hospital is no longer there, replaced by high rise condominiums.

A nurse knocked on my door and asked if I wanted to go on a smoke break. I said sure, then followed her to the nurse's station where she dispensed one cigarette to each of us, then chose a lighter which we would all share. As I waited with the group by the elevator, I noticed this guy who was cursing under his breath and saying how much he hated it here and he was going to escape the first chance he got. (There is one of those in every crowd at the hospital). He seemed very angry and agitated, and capable of violence. He made me feel very uncomfortable. As we exited the building, the heat washed over us like opening a hot oven door. The nurse directed us to the center of the parking lot where there were two chairs and a cement block. We all lit up.

Then, suddenly, a man who had been rocking back and forth on the cement block, started singing in Italian - Opera. He had an incredible voice and his song had a rhythm and flow to it. The man who had made me feel so uncomfortable softened considerably and silently extended his hands out to me. As I approached him, he place one hand on my hip and gently clasp my hand with his other hand. We settled in close to one another and started to slow dance - being careful not to singe each others' hair with our cigarettes. The nurse did not stop us. I laid my head on his shoulder, followed his steps, and listened to this man's entrancing voice. The nurse allowed us to continue past the allotted break time.

When the man stopped singing, my dance partner leaned in toward me and whispered, "Run away with me", then backed away. I shook my head no and said, "I can't- I am not able to". I never saw or heard of him again.
I found out later that the singer had autism.

This slow dance to the vocals of a talented singer, in the intense heat, in the shadow of a psychiatric hospital, with a cigarette balanced in my fingers, and in the embrace of a stranger felt bizarre and sad, and defiant but also hopeful. It was the sprinkle of magic that gave me hope to get through this particular bout of depression.

Where I Try Again

I go kicking and screaming - at least in my mind. A silent ambulance ride takes me far from my home. I arrive feeling embarrassed that I am here once again. The doors lock behind me; I am not allowed to go. They take away my shoelaces, my belt, and cell phone. A thorough inventory is taken of my limited possessions. A pocketknife found in my purse prompts a humiliating strip search. My purse is taken away with money and any other valuables - including my jewelry. I am subjected to probing questions about my state of mind and history. I tell what I can of my story given my current state of mind. My hand shakes uncontrollably while I sign endless forms. I am watched closely for signs of a death wish and trying to end my life. From the time of admission to the time I leave, discharge plans are made. My initial thoughts are to kill myself upon release - this is just a temporary pause and inconvenience.

I'm given hotel sized soap, shampoo, conditioner, lotion, deodorant, toothbrush, toothpaste, and a towel. When I finally take a shower, there is a loud, startling knock on the door, "Are you all right?" I imagine smashing the mirror and cutting myself with the pieces - but it is metal and would only bend.

Patients are here due to grief, depression, and madness. Some say they'll try to escape, some say they will hurt themselves, others quietly gaze into space. Most of them, like me, are biding their time until they feel stronger. My experience here is not unique.

The bed is a lumpy slab of rock, so instead of sleeping, I

listen to the activities of the night: hushed conversations and the clack on keyboards as nurses file reports, frightening screams and sorrowful crying heard from other rooms, and my roommate's moaning and sighs turn to snoring, as I lay awake in the dark. Hourly the door creeks opened, splashing the room with light. An attendant peaks in quietly to see if I'm dead or alive. I roll over and stare out the window etched with foul words and "HELP!". It is a relief to know I am safe here from myself. At least, this is what I choose to believe. And I could kill for a cigarette or two.

Morning, sleepy-eyed, a nurse yells to line up for vital signs (weigh-in, blood pressure, pulse, and temperature). The ward is coming alive. The smell of fresh coffee wafts from the nurses' station- but we are only allowed decaf. The phones are locked and unavailable until after group times. Shuffling, heavily medicated stockers of the hallway utter words of a secret language. An unsympathetic nurse scolds me for sleeping on the couch. Sleeping? That's hilarious. Shivering, I wait for meds and the breakfast cart to arrive.

Everything is scheduled - sleeping, eating, therapy, medications, visiting, and smoking. I wait eagerly for the cigarette breaks like a true nicotine addict.

I am exhausted and depressed - I only want to sleep and be left alone - but that is not allowed. Participation in tedious Group therapy is mandatory. "What is it that brought you here?" asked several times to medicated patients with blank unknowing stares. Do they mean to ask "What is your story?" again to people who are barely conscious?

I think sarcastically - it must be the pleasant atmosphere, gourmet food, lessons on coping, how to spend time productively, and crafts that keep me from killing myself in here - right. At least, they are temporary distractions from the torture within. The hours pass slowly, painfully, as I desire to be in familiar places. I think, "I actually pay for this torture?" But I know I could not be safe and free at the same time yet.

Plopping down in front of me, an unfamiliar eager listener (probably the ink on her diploma hasn't dried yet), with pen and notepad, spends time with me. Trying to work a puzzle with missing and broken pieces. Wirily I tell my story again, negativity pervades; and the pen flies across several pages, creating a written record of my misery. I see my sadness reflected in her eyes. I would dictate my life's story to each new health care worker who talked to me. Couldn't they share notes? She sincerely promises that we will talk again, but we never do.

Three times a day, I try to stomach hospital food. I have no appetite, but it is something to do.
In the evenings, the phones are unlocked. The angry, tearful conversations of other patients make me nervous and are overheard by everyone. Worried, frightened visitors come to spend time with their loved one. Bored children run and scream down the halls. I occasionally have a visitor - only a couple of people know I am here.

The TV is on; just a few hours are allowed in the evening. Nightly, there is a struggle over control of the remote and what program we will watch - I leave and go to my room - I can't handle the drama.
Once or twice I see the Psychiatrist. He stares at me with

analytical eyes and asks me to tell my story again- he must wonder why I look annoyed and violent (it must be a look he is accustomed to). In his hand, is the binder that holds the notes from all the staff members that have talked to or observed me. He determines if changes to my medications are in order. Appointments are made with outpatient groups and a therapist. And the date for my return to work is decided.

Several days later, when I feel much improved - no longer victimized by my own mind, I make my departure of this place, vowing to never return. The bill is tabulated, cross-referenced, and mailed - A sweet surprise in my mailbox. In the sterile sunlight, I wait for a cab to take me back to the clinic where my car is parked. During the ride, familiar places pass before my newly focused eyes. When we enter the parking lot, I see my car on the left, third from the end – my old friend. I give the driver my voucher and tip, start my vehicle, and head home. As I pause beside my house, fear turns to hope. I will succeed. I have to. I know I can.

Home is where I try again.

CHAPTER 3 - BEFORE DAWN

Reaching for the Dawn

As a child, I lay awake fearing this would be the night he would come to take me away from my bed and go to the study, where we would play his sickening games.

As I waited, cars passed by on the street below; things in my room cast shadows on the walls appearing to me like frightening monsters.

My eyes were focused on the space under the door. When the hall light came on, I heard the creaking of the hard wood floors and the sound of my father's ankles popping, then the slow turning of the door knob; I knew it was time. My heart raced and I began to whimper as he took my little hand and quietly lead me down the hall.

I prayed for daylight because I knew he only came for me in the middle of the night, when everyone else was sleeping deeply.

I have survived these long years because I never stopped reaching from the darkness to the dawn. It holds for me the hope that a new day could mean a different day. I believed that, if I could hang on, I will be strong enough for change and it will be glorious and healing.

A Slender Leaf

A slender leaf turns gray and falls in the faint moonlight.
Gloom fills my soul and shades my mood tonight.
A child's giggles become frightening sounds in the dark.
Emotional pain is unbearable and leaves a noticeable
mark.

Depression envelops me like a cloak of prickly thorns.
My confidence is shaken, broken and torn.
Favorite meals taste like paste mixed with sand.
Flowers have no fragrance and wilt in my hand.

Reality is distorted and things are not as they appear.
An expression of self-destruction whispers in my ear.
I feel more dead than alive and I want to be alone.
A gray, slender leaf tumbles in the wind and is gone.

Daddy's Little Girl

You called me "Daddy's Little Girl" for a while.
When I touched you there and took off my underwear.
I was too young and scared but you made me smile.
Obeying your commands, I caressed you everywhere.
Not crying because I was numb to it all.
Not telling because I was ashamed of myself.
The only witnesses were asleep down the hall.
Silently you kept me close to yourself.
Now, I can't trust enough to love anyone.
Now, I feel like my life is undone?
But I'm trying to get over it; the pain's nearly gone.
Surely, Daddy, you have not won.
So don't try to call me "Daddy's Little Girl" again.
I don't want to see you for the rest of my lifespan.

I Heard A Cry for Help

In a dream, I heard a cry for help –
    it was sad and urgent and pleading.
I wanted to find this person and help them with the
    agony they were feeling.
The crying sounds were gripping and suffocating.
But the voice was too distant and soft to be located.

In a dream, I heard a cry for help –
    it was something I heard before.
Panic ensued and I did not want to experience this dream
    anymore.
The cries were coming from inside me now expressed in
    wordless thoughts.
A feeling from within, a desire to live,
    and time I thought I had bought.

It was a fight to overcome, a push to save my life,
    and a desire to be free.
I was the one who needed help –
    I must save myself from me.

Black Tar Stick Men

Driving home from work alone through the dense and pulsating darkness- I hear only the sounds of my weary old car and it's substandard radio playing some "Golden Oldie" through irritating static.

Then the black tar patches covering cracks in the pavement peel from the dark road and stretch their rubbery forms into tall spiked stick men reaching for me. They seemed alive and angry - changing form and getting taller.

I say, "I am not seeing this- right?" Trying to convince myself. I squint my tired eyes and turn to look again. Now, they are flat on the street as they should be. As they always were.

Dark Figures

Dark figure embraces a shiny lamppost.
What is he doing there?

Dark figure sits on the bus stop bench
Watching me pass by.

Dark figure runs before my low beams.
I frantically crush the brakes.

Dark figure appears in the passenger seat
Patiently riding beside me.

Dark figures, night time illusions
Cause temporary confusions.
When sunlight plays in the meadows,
Dark figures recede in the shadows.

In My Dark House

In my dark house,
Cold illumination rising.
Demons watch with red tumid eyes.

Alone but not safe
No solace in stillness.

Emotions turn, a violent stimulation.
Thoughts spill, rank and insistent.
Muscles flaccid on ice.

Dreams lost in times remembered -
An annoying secondhand rhythm
No time for anything but wasting time.

Scenarios of the end play
Checking for errors.

As demons watch with red tumid eyes,
I wait for the warm illumination rising
In my dark house.

Depression is a Foul Killing Poison

Sadness pushes deep inside me,
    as lazy hot vapors spill from my throat -
    tightened from tears unbroken.
Squeezed tighter still from the difficult words left
    unspoken.
Depression is a foul killing poison oozing from every
    pore.
It steals the color from my world and makes all my
    senses dull.
Simple tasks take a heroic effort like climbing endlessly
    uphill.
I enjoy nothing - no time to be enthusiastic-
    only to be still.
Hallucinations, dreams, and reality mix in a frightful
    battle of wills.
I cannot prioritize because everything is equally
    unimportant –
    most things are delayed indefinitely or
    forgotten completely.
The sunshine - with it's painful brightness and
    unbearable endless burning,
    is like a large silent dancing clown
    with heavy makeup dripping.
    It is annoying because it brings no joy or
    pleasantness - only suffocating.
When the night comes, I get some relief.
To be still, so still, in the dark where I lie-
where no one knows I listen, watch, and cry.

A Shining Knight

A shining Knight has emerged from the mists to re-kindle
a flame from long ago.
Release regrets and inhibitions – feel free to explore and
let go.

Your dreams and fantasies have created a beautiful
mosaic of comfortable protection.
But the Knight sparks a re-awakening of lust and desire
that demands your immediate attention.

Let romance be the candle that flickers in your eyes.
Allow anticipation to rival that of your youth.
Trust your pounding heart for it won't lead you far from
the seductive truth.

May love find its way into your welcoming soul, making a
home with your history, the present and future.
The news of your love will pass between the
constellations afar - bound with cosmic adhesive for two.

And when it settles in, your love will be accented by hot,
colorful fireworks; but also pleasant and safe like a chair
that cradles you perfectly, an adorable animal in your lap,
a hot cup of coffee to your lips, and a smile that tells of
the thoughts within.

CHAPTER 4 - MAY I BE EXCUSED

The Anger, the Rage

When rage fills my heart, I cannot escape; it engulfs me and takes over my thoughts. I fight this feeling of hatred; I think of other things in my life, but there are many problems. I can't seem to remember the good in the world and within myself. Bad thoughts crush my brain; I can't concentrate, I can't reason, I can't stand it, I can't survive. I am afraid to be alone with my thoughts. I want to keep my mind and body occupied so that I won't think about anything disturbing. When I am alone, it seems that the only way to avoid these thoughts is to hurt myself, so I do as much damage as possible. I can't bear the idea of hurting anyone who may be close to me by killing myself, but I need to do something.

Some Things About Me

I am a compassionate leader and loyal follower,
I am honest, sometimes to a fault.
I care deeply about people and their sorrows.
To "love thy neighbor" is what I was taught.

Children should learn and grow at their own pace.
Not forced to do things they have nightmares about.
Not coerced to do things they cannot erase.
And later in life, about living, have their doubts.

I am shy, not self-confident, around men I don't know.
I don't feel very good about my appearance for dating.
I don't know how others see me - what I show.
It's a major stumbling block to mating.

And I can't get over the trust issue either.
How can I tell if he would be abusive?
I don't know if he is a good fit for me either.
And a relationship I don't want is intrusive.

I believe I will never make it to old age and be free.
So far, I have had the courage to go on with it.
But each depression takes more and more out of me.
I would like to die young and be done with it.

Depression Below the Lifeline

When a depression dips below the lifeline,
When I am lost and frightened and in pain,
My face darkens and sags from the weight of it.
My throat clenches - words are hard to say.

When no longer frightened,
but determined to make it happen,
there is no contact with others,
no further effort to stop.
I change course and
prepare to carry out my plan.
People will just have to understand
that I did the best I could,
But could no longer tolerate the deep, unending pain.
I am very sorry -
my broken heart cannot explain.

When depression dips below the death line
The fight is over, all have lost -
I've given up despite the cost
Drowning in sorrow,
I picture your beloved faces
This will hurt loved ones deeply
so I give your hearts embraces.
Then I exit without a word, or a whimper,
or a scream. Just a long exhale.

Time One Thousand and One

Uncomfortable in my own skin, but where else can I go?
Redundant lyrics to distant love songs -
I sing sadly the words I know.

My happiness is not stronger than a thousand melancholy tears.
No one knows my inner turmoil - they only see my fear.

When I express a desire to die in rhymes,
They laugh, "We've heard that a thousand times".

My sadness is gossip passed between village rooftops.
So I will travel that rocky trail to a majestic mountaintop.

I will simply go without saying, "I want to die" for time one thousand and one.
Sparing myself the embarrassment of their laughter, I head out toward the sun.

The mountains ahead are held tight by dark rolling thunder clouds,
They are towering high, a beautiful sight, powerful, and proud.

Creatures of the mountain are both frightened away and bold.
Birds, frantic from the impending storm, watch the terrible scene unfold.

My breath comes in labored gasps as I ascend the trail to the top.
A dense, gray mist pushes through the Pines like spirits urging me to stop.

The bubbling river in the valley below, silently waits to swallow me whole.
It's time to end this crazy dance and go to the Ball with my soul.

So I jump as lightening splits the sky and, I finally, feel free of my skin.
The air races passed me and panic grips my heart, but time is stretched very thin.

As the earth reaches up to claim my body, I realize I am done.
And darkness ascends and darkness descends and nothing is nothing.

I am gone forever. No chance for time one thousand and one.
...and the pain is almost gone.

Again

Again, I am in turmoil-
    struggling to keep working-
    struggling to hide my weakness from family-
    trying to appear okay to everyone-
    trying to keep moving and doing.
Crying wet sloppy tears behind my eyes where no one can see.

I choke on my breath and it seems my heart beats only occasionally.

I feel like I haven't had a month's worth of sleep (yet I know I've slept some).

I don't have any room or strength for disappointment or emotional upset.

I am in a dream like fog-

nothing seems real.

I feel very close to not trying anymore-
    not caring anymore-
    not being at all.

The Fabric, My Fabric

Is the fabric of my life woven with a strong, tight weave-
    yet soft and smooth, like silk, to the touch?

Do the colors and patterns reflect my taste, preferences,
    and personality?

Maybe one time, long ago, I caught a glimpse of how it
    could be- how it was supposed to be.

And it was unfamiliar and out of reach,
    so I rejected it.

Instead, my life's fabric has many missing pieces,
    seams that don't fit together,
    holes with badly frayed edges,
    and the colors have washed out and faded.

The fabric is rough like concrete and smells like smoke
    and dirt.

The best thing for this fabric would be to incinerate it.

In the End

Would you talk to me on my blackest day, though I may
not respond at all?
> Or would you quickly retreat to save yourself,
>> Not able to witness the deepest of my pain?

Would you wait for me at the edge of darkness as I try to
find my way back?
> Or would you leave me at the side of the road and
> wish me well?
>> Not having the patience for me to return.

Will you believe in me when I have lost all hope for
myself?
> Or would you concede that I am lost and turn your
> back on me?
>> Will you agree that enough has been tried -
>> it's time to give up?

Would you have the courage to stand on the side of life as
I urgently reject it?
> And would you gently help pull me away from a
> wrongful early death?
>> Do you think less of me because of the
>> dark, fatal journey I take?

In the end, in reality, it does not matter so much what
you do for me or think of me- what matters is what I
think and do for myself.

Because, in the end, I stand on every road and shore -

alone. No one to hold me, just my own courage, the desire to learn self love, and the drive to embrace survival.

Thank you

This dance with death is an obscene waltz.
I step on my own toes as I try to find my way.
Through the dense fog hope seems false.
Death was on my doorstep, a few steps away.
Obsessed with dying to escape what was rough,
I conspired to harm myself by setting aside pills.
Waiting and wondering how much would be enough
to end my life, end the pain - was my only will.
Like a whisper in the dark, you tried to make it right.
You helped me realize that I needed help urgently.
You made me give up the means of ending my life.
And saved, not just me, but also my entire family.
I don't want to hurt anyone, but to live I have a
serious objection.
So thank you for guiding me in the right direction.

CHAPTER 5 - HOPE BLOSSOMS

Comfort and Support Is

Comfort is a warm blanket we wrap around those we love to protect them against a violent, freezing storm.

Love is wanting to be a beacon for each other when finding the way becomes frightening, confusing, and dark.

Love in sickness is to hold out your hand in support, make sacrifices and compromises, without making judgments or feeling shame - but to help this person feel loved and as whole as possible.

Love is letting the people you love know how you feel-often.

And when a healing loved one becomes strong enough to shed that warm cozy blanket, rejoice in their quest to redefine themselves - and only remain close enough to cheer them on and catch them if they falter.

With the Sunrise

With the sunrise, the birds come out to sing and play.

Sunshine heals- with nutrient effects on your mind, body,
and soul.

In the sunlight, beauty is seen with vibrant color and
wonder.

The start of a new day holds the possibility that things
can get better and I will do what I can to make that
happen.

In the morning sunlight, I turn my face to the sky
and pray that the ones I love have a fabulous day.

For Someone Like Me

For someone like me who:
Cries inside for the child that lost her innocence too soon.
And who sees frightening images of the abuse that
occurred.
And feels the guilt and shame from her "willing"
participation.

For someone like me who:
Clings to a hatred of her father
And who rejects the idea of forgiveness
And feels an overwhelming anxiety when he is nearby.

For someone like me who:
Held her mother's hand into death
And who wished to go with her
And grieved for the loss of her favorite earthly being.

For someone like me who:
Struggles with self-esteem
Tries to carry the weight of the world on her shoulders
And places too much importance on her job.

For someone like me who:
When feeling emotionally numb, cut into her flesh.
And who wished to feel more alive by doing so
And was able to get relief, but left scares.

For someone like me who:
Sometimes feels the pain of depression so severely

That she wants to or attempts to take her own life
And her love of family and friends is not enough.

For someone like me who:
Struggles with health issues
And should do more exercise
And eat much healthier.

For someone like me who:
Occasionally has hypomania
And who spends too much money
And gets hyperactive, works too much,
doesn't sleep, doesn't eat.

For someone like me who:
Needed help and received help with these issues and
more.

Thank God there was someone like you.

Healing Again

I rise into peace feeling wounded, but healing
The world around me less bleak.
Nightmares of depression left me disbelieving
Recovery was possible for me.

With help, I made it through another episode.
Heightened senses cannot be ignored.
A mind lightened from such a heavy load
Is free to think beautiful thoughts, not bored.

And love, a concept, unfamiliar and broken
Has renewed meaning and a life of its own.
The healing words I need to speak are spoken.
I know now I don't have to do this alone.

And this time around I feel I have won.
I stand here with my soul wanting to soar.
Like a flower opening its arms to the sun
I enthusiastically embrace life once more.

Touch Me

Touch me, Life, with your golden light.
Fill my senses with wondrous intensity.
Give me experiences to live a lifetime right,
And the strength to get through animosity.

Touch me; Hope, with your cool blue glow.
Give me strength to greet each new day.
Let goals, and dreams of the future flow.
Give me peace of mind, to be free today.

Touch me, Happiness, with your uplifting purple.
Let me find joy in things, big and small.
Fill my days with laughter and one less hurdle.
Give me courage to seek things I like, not appall.

Touch me; Love, with your rich red hue.
Let me reach beyond limits in intimacy.
To trust and not fear relationships I'm due-
Express love of others and self enthusiastically.

Was It You There

Was it you there sitting beside me in the night?
Who whispered, "Your history will soon take flight".
Those others will come to know me well
Who never thought twice to notice me there?

Was it you there listening to my nightmares
With a concerned look and a tremble in your lips.
The words I said were not easy to say or hear.
They bore witness to a man's cruelty to a woman.

Was it you there who took my hand and held it strong:
Encouraging me to walk through thorny fields
That scratched my arms and legs and face
In order to overcome and emerge free from self-torture.

Is it you who believes in the power in me
To honor the past but set it aside
And live my life – every hour, every day
By accumulating positive experiences and minimizing the
other.

How the Healing Began

Driven wild by panic on the wheels of flaming electricity.
My heart was in a devil's race to find its way or self-
 destruct.

My heart pounded loud and rhythmic like sneakers
 bumping around in the dryer.

A trusted friend saw me struggling, turned her back, and
 walked away.
No help to be had; I was on my own.

With a broken self-esteem, I pictured myself as an
 undesirable monster - forever alone.

With no frame of reference for reality, hallucinations
 blocked the way to comfort and sanity.

You can't stick an ice pack on hurt feelings, emotions, or
 mental illness.

It takes a magical combination of medication, therapy,
time, and the desire to be well.

Then, when I felt safe, I broke my silence and began to
 tell my story.

Remarkably, things in my world didn't start blowing up -
 like I was sure they would.

I told my story verbally to trusted people and I wrote

about my experiences.

It helped me remember, it helped me purge, and it helped me heal and forget.

It also allowed me to re-shape my identity and re-write my future path.

Then hope was a word I could speak out loud and believe in.

So I carried on for those I love and those I don't even know;

But most important, I did it for me -
For change in myself is more permanent and meaningful when under my control.

Reaching Out to Me

I feel your hand reaching out to me in the dark
    and it gives me some hope while I struggle there.
Life is full of surprises, stresses, and worries-
    good, fantastic things too.
It helps to not keep score of things that have gone wrong.
I try not to worry about the future because it is fortune
telling and I don't have that talent to a reliable degree.
I need all my energy to deal with the present.

Give Life Another Try

Take comfort in the quiet night-
Let sleep heal your aching wounds.
With it you can conquer mountains,
Without it you may play the fool.
Leave behind in the murky shadows-
Your worries, anger and fears.
Take in the sunlight as it paints the warm morning sky.
A new day is a perfect chance to give life another try.

The Ceramic Mug

I was going thru my kitchen cupboards and I ran across this white ceramic coffee mug with blue antique accenting. It is very old and symbolizes a lot to me. I painted this mug when I was 19 yrs old and in a psych hospital for the first time. I was so overwhelmed that year. So much was happening. My mind and body broke down; and I went from wishing I could die to trying to make it happen. It was a couple of weeks after my first suicide attempt, about a month after the rape, several months after the voice started, and about a year after my sister told me about being molested by my father for 10 years.

I painted this mug when I was in shock and in a mental haze where I was not real, and no one around me was real, and people talked to me as if from far away. I made this cup because it represented hope for me that things would get better and it was proof to myself that I still existed even though I felt quite dead.

Now, I look at this ugly old mug and I think to myself that the tiny spark of hope I had back then was a big part of what has kept me alive all these years in addition to not wanting to hurt anyone. I think I will keep this mug.

You've given me a hand.

You are my friend and you've given me a hand.
Your encouragement enables me to get up and
stand.

I have been stronger because you've been there
to cheer.
When blinded by darkness, you lead me through
fear.

And when I struggle to meet each new day.
You remind me tomorrow will be okay.

You are my friend and you've given me a hand.
So, when time moves as slow as grains of sand.

When life's got you down with stress and strife,
Look back and I will give you a tour of your life.

The happy, giddy times when you laughed until
you cried.
And everything was light and easy and a joyful ride.

The End of Therapy

Remind me now why I was here
Why I told you my secrets and fears
Why I spent years trying to find myself
In the reflections of a human mirror.
My sickened heart has finally leapt forward
To melt away into golden valleys
To become part of a beautiful world once hidden
Behind tears, nightmares, and things askew.
To remember a life lived despite the pain
Where I laughed, and created, and loved
Now I cross a bridge alone, but free
To be happy, and brave, and alive

CHAPTER 6 - RELATIONSHIPS

A Wish of Love for Everyone

My view of love is that it is many faceted, many layered, and filled with vibrant color, like a deep red rose. Out of love and kindness come peace and contentment. Not to say that love will eliminate problems, but that, with love you can get through anything together.

Love starts with yourself. If you have self-love and self-esteem, then you can give love honestly to others and receive love without question. Self acceptance leads to self love and should be practiced.

The love of children is like no other love in the universe and is above all else - from birth through a lifetime and beyond. The love of a mother or father for their son or daughter is something that makes the air thick with sweetness - and makes the people looking on feel warm and smile.

Love of your parents. They were our grand teachers about life and, hopefully, we learned the right lessons from them. Parents also teach you what it means to be strong, caring, respectful, and responsible. The parent-child relationship can sometimes evolve into a close friendship, which makes that bond stronger and beautiful.

Love of a spouse and the mutual love given in return gives you the opportunity to live, dream, and plan with a life partner. **Romantic love** is what makes us feel so good about ourselves, about our world, and our place in it. It is where we learn the importance of both giving and receiving love. And **passionate love** is what makes our eyes shine, our toes curl, makes our bodies respond, makes us lose our minds a little, and leaves us begging for more.

Love of siblings. Most of the time these individuals were present when you were a child and as you became an adult. They were witnesses to some of the things you experienced. And, as a family, you learned most of the same things. Siblings may be the ones you go to when you need to talk.

Love of friends. You choose to be with and talk to these people because they understand you and your life circumstances. They are there for you when, sometimes, no one else is. They listen and give advice when they can, help you feel better about yourself, they don't judge you or your family, they help when it is appropriate, and let you know it is okay to laugh and be silly or to cry.

Love of pets. Whether they be dogs or cats, birds or hamsters, lizards or snakes- they have simple needs, they are not that demanding - most just want to be petted and fed and given a safe environment. The petting brings us a healing calm and they make good company when there is no one else around. Most are considered valued members of the family.

Love and kindness lead to peace, happiness, and contentment. Make a life accented with compassion and doing the "right thing" for others. Have more awareness and expression of the love you feel. And let the last thing heard or said be "I Love You".

When You Are Near

Whenever you are near,
My shyness disappears,
No more sadness or fear.
Instead, there is a warm glow in my eyes.
Caution and reserve replaced with a smile.
Laughter and confidant exchanges for awhile.
Your voice vibrates throughout my inner core-
It's distracting, calming, and I want for more.
My feet are barely holding the floor.
Imagination fills with magical moments with you.
Evening light splashes the room with azure blue.
Touches subtle and not so subtle too.
Our ages differ, but we are not worlds apart.
A friendship with you is where I'd like to start.
But deeper still there is a longing in my heart.
I feel like I have always known you.
Take my hand and I will go with you.
Come to me if you are of like mind and soul
And we will see how large a love can grow.

His Special Place

In the hot noon sun, not a cloud in the sky, we retrieve our backpacks from the back of his car. He says I will enjoy this hike through the desert to a secret place he found. We start along the path as a small lizard scurries by. The crunch of our steps is echoed through the small sand-colored canyon. He is an experienced hiker so the walk is at a fast pace. I am in good shape, but after a while, I want a break. When we finally stop for a drink of water from our canteens, I wonder how long this will take. We start again, and soon I am dizzy from the overwhelming heat. No longer enjoying the view around me, I focus on the path ahead, taking each step at a time, and trying not to pass out. And just when I am ready to ask to stop completely and turn back, we arrive at this secluded area. There is a slab of rock with sand, like beach sand, all around and the Colorado River passing nearby. I could hear the soothing sound of rushing water.

We put down our backpacks, took a sip of water, and explored his hidden wonder. There are cactus and desert flowers everywhere. The canyon walls are a mix of color – yellow, tans, white, orange, black, and red. The river, at this junction, is very wide and green (probably algae). The water rushes over boulders in the middle creating a layer of white water and water running in several directions.

Hungry, we set up the small Sterno stove, heat up some stew, and enjoy dinner with oranges. There is some wine for the occasion. We smile at one another and talk. I turn on the tape player we brought, playing light romantic love songs. We clean up the plates and small pot in the sand, then hold each other and kiss, his rough stubble scratching my skin. The sunset over the canyon is brilliant with color - we sit and watch holding hands. I feel very close to him.

He got up and said he needed to go to the bathroom. Taking the flashlight, he disappears around a rock ledge. And while he is gone, I unzip our sleeping bags, placing mine on the bottom and his on the top. The sun has gone down and the clean desert air has become breezy and chilly. I get under the sleeping bag to warm up. What is taking him so long? I began to feel comfortable and warm. Roberta Flack's "The First Time Ever I Saw Your Face" echoes softly in the night air. I promptly fall into a deep sleep.

In the middle of the night, I wake up and realize I had been asleep for a while. In a panic, I sit upright and look around. There he is sleeping next to me. I curse myself for falling asleep on such a romantic night. I tentatively call his name and pat his back, but he does not stir. I feel disappointed knowing that this would have been a special night for both of us. I lie back down; awake until dawn, and watch a thousand stars wink at me. Hoping that he would be understanding and we would laugh about it.

In the morning, I sense anger, as he gives me the silent treatment. I try to make small talk, but he just ignores me. I apologize for having fallen asleep and ask why he didn't wake me. Still silent. After eating a granola bar and another orange, we gather our things for the hike back to the car. The return trip is much faster and more comfortable without the heat of the afternoon sun. He says we will go for a swim in the lake before heading home. At least there is a public bathroom there, however disgusting, it was still a welcomed sight. I had been "holding it" through much of the night. He swims with his back toward me. I feel rejected and scorned for no good reason. He took too long returning (what in the heck was he doing?) and he didn't wake me up when he returned, which would have been fine with me. And he didn't respond when I tried to wake him up.

During the drive home, he finally speaks saying that he isn't really mad at me. He feels that our perfect night was cut short by me even though it was not my fault. But he thinks if it really were important, I would have found a way to stay awake. I say that I don't think it was something I could have controlled – and it seemed like he was gone for a long time. I point out that there surely would be other opportunities. He agrees but the ride home is silent and still feels uncomfortable.

To Let a Relationship Start

Bees don't fly in the pouring rain;
and I don't come out of my nest.
To look for love or companionship -
to hide - I think it is best.
I cling to the idea, "I am happy alone",
Keeps me going while my interest is gone.

It's unfamiliar territory to trust someone with my
heart.
I'm too independent and single of habit
to let a relationship start.

But, now I want to hold a strong man's hand.
He can make me feel safe and
I can be his best fan.
I want him to be honest, caring, and kind.
With a passion for living that will change my mind.

I want to share all of myself - and not stay trapped alone.
And find love in its purest form with happiness that comes
along.
To come out of my shell and be a different person -
One who engages life instead of hiding from its pleasures.

I'm Stuck

The beginning is an Internet discovery.
A revealing email is just a preliminary.
Foreplay is through our mutual machinery.
Fearing a virus, our movement is cautionary.

You remove software from a jewel case dramatically.
The game commences pressing buttons frantically.
Our keyboards light up; interactive binary.
My desktop displays you in High Definition with beautiful scenery.

I've downloaded your pixels and shared your memory.
A review of my files takes longer than customary.
There are errors in our relationship apparently.
Irritating pop ups say you're not even ordinary.

Are we compatible? A disappointing summary displays.
Trying to contact you, my device freezes indifferently.
I'm stuck. Soft boot. I try again fervently.
Still no response.
Hard boot. It's over - definitely.

It's Time

I desire a richness of life that is possible only when it is
shared.
Majestic views of mountaintops and streams are best
seen as a pair.

Sunrises and sunsets are meant as lovers' lights.
I have traveled far too long on my solitary flight.

Now, I will turn back for home and change my direction.
Old memories are history – time to make a new
connection.

I want to laugh and see my smile reflected in his eyes.
I want to hold his hand and gaze upon the starry skies.

It's time to stop and smell the roses again.
And it's time I was back in the arms of a loving man.

Divided Highway

Driving on a moonless, pitch dark night - even the stars
seemed dim:
    The road is rough and not well cared for and makes
      my car bounce.
        I should turn on my lights,
        But I am afraid of the future ahead.

Driving much too fast - speed signs are a blur along the
empty highway:
    My car still bounces along the uneven payment
    only faster.
        I should slow down,
        But I don't want the past to catch up.

Repeatedly glancing in the foggy, rearview mirror -
    I know something frightful is following me just
    over the horizon:
        I suppose I should relax,
        There is nothing there.

I keep missing the highway exits – so my destination
eludes me:
    I turn around and try the approach again and again.
        I must concentrate harder,
        But my thoughts are confused.

Dreaming still dreaming about love – any love:
        I should stop torturing myself,
        Because I want one so badly.

When I got tired and ran out of gas alone on the divided highway, I heard a rumble in the distance. And as it approached, headlights lit up the sky over a distant hill, my body trembled and my heart raced. A car stopped on the road not far from me and someone got out and walked toward me. As this person came into focus, I realized that I had been running from myself; she was just standing there, smiling; she was the part of me that had been missing for so long. I stood up and she hugged me, and I promised to get to know her again.

And, as I walked back to my car, I looked out onto the divided highway and watched it merge into one long straight road leading to home. And I felt warm and relieved in the glow of sunrise. Love was restored and now I could continue my journey.

Dear Friend

I see you as if standing alone in a cold, dark rain -
shivering.
Not a nourishing rain, but punishing, painful, icy.
Heaving shoulders and screaming, "Why?"
Life has been unkind to one who likes to smile so much.
If warm thoughts could comfort someone in pain,
If I could take away the sorrow and keep it at bay,
If I could make right what has gone terribly wrong,
If I could hug your heart so you know you are loved,
I would do all that and more if I could.
Alas, my magical gifts for healing are limited.
But if listening, caring, and praying is what I can do,
Then I will do my very best for you.

Did I Leave Something There Last Night?

Hey, did I leave something there last night?
Not in the open but not out of sight.
It might have been lost when you turned out the light.
When your arms wrapped around me and held me so
tight.

Is it under rumpled sheets next to smelly socks?
Did you take it with you on that midnight sleepwalk?
Maybe on the dresser under your worn cap?
Between dusty bookshelves, hiding in the gap?

Or beneath that moist, yellow towel on the floor?
Behind your gray bathrobe nailed to the door?
Mixed with dirty laundry shoved over there?
By the foggy window at the top of the stairs?

I'm thinking. Aren't you, of where it might be?
Can you look? It's important and precious to me.
Oh wait! Here it is! It was here all along.
I lost myself in your world, and stayed much too long.

A Shy Timid Part of Me

A shy timid part of me revealed itself today.
It peaked so reluctantly from behind a desert tree,
To watch me say good-bye to you as I fought to smile, not sigh;
Believing that I'd see you again, made it easy for a while.

A long, full hug was not enough to keep you from departing.
Boarding the plane, you disappeared - the engine now was starting.
With a heaving chest and a lump in my throat, I tried to be brave.
I wanted to scream, "Come back"; but all I could do was wave.

Then I passed the threshold of my resistance,
The lump in my throat turned to liquid.
It spilled through my eyes and rolled down my cheeks-
The shy timid part of me glistened.

In Fall, I Think of You

In Fall, colorful leaves protest the dimming of light,
temperatures are mild, and breezes are slight.
Before snow paints the mountains in white -
Make love to me under the sparkling moonlight.

Shadows from the past move, come to life, and glow.
I smile and touch you from balding head to curled up toe.
Getting lost in your steel blue eyes while tears begin to
flow.
My shaking hands follow contours of your long familiar
frame.
Your deep, soulful voice makes me purr in a thrilling
wicked game.
I want to be wrapped in the comfort of you for eternity.
Your early death cheated us both of days in blissful unity.

I lost you in the Fall and remember you most then.
My love has not died, it lives in memories of when.
My dreaming mind is a playground of dangerous, lustful
romance.
But I do not fear your gentle spirit -
so caress me with your loving hands.
I long to feel your hot, steamy breath
as you whisper soft golden words in my ear.
Make me believe you are here for a while- brush away my
sadness and tears.

When the magic of the night quickly fades away,
I must let you go until that special Fall day

When colorful leaves protest the dimming of light,
temperatures are mild, and breezes are slight.
When colorful leaves float gently to the ground,

And I, I am waiting - eager and earthbound.

CHAPTER 7 - LIFE HAPPENS TOO

Flailing Arms

Flailing arms and rightly so.
A fragrant candle's gentle glow.

What right do I have to know-
The order of books stacked in a row?

Neighbors' shouts - whispered distant and low -
Go unnoticed beyond screams of our own

Rocky lawns, no need to mow-
Yellowed but once were white as snow

Children crying down below-
Listen to their ages grow

Trying to leave, he did not go-
Honey's gone and jammed his toe

A wind, blown backwards, does not blow.
Even electricity seems too slow.
Now I know to just say "no"
And wrap it with a golden bow.

Just Another Day

A rude alarm, and loneliness echoes across the perfect
room.
Dressing darkly with old clothes to match my solemn
mood.
A caffeine fix for imitation enthusiasm.
A white-knuckled commute on the jammed highway to
work.
Trying to solve problems that have no solution
Trying to please people who will not be satisfied
Exhausted on the ride home, but a moment to reflect
Just another day wrapped in rusty ribbon, presented with
a crooked smile.

A sunrise with blazing color outside my window east,
Lounging in comfortable clothes reading the daily news.
A weekend breakfast with eggs, a bagel, and juice,
A brisk walk through the park invigorates the mind and
body
Finding time for only the pleasant things to do.
Moments pass sweetly without room for distress
And time well spent is time kept as a fond memory.
Just another day wrapped in golden ribbon, Presented
with a glowing smile.

The Music

A car pulls up beside me at an intersection.
Loud vibrations, from that car, shake the ground, nearby
cars, and homes – Earthquake Music that might even
make the pen on the Richter scale wiggle.

It is an enticing, thumping, heavy bass, and irritating
repetitive beat. Some drivers hold completely still as if
there is no noise happening. The driver bounces in his
seat and gyrates to the rhythm. He seems to be having a
really good time.

But has really he listened to the words he is screaming?
Cursing, killing, men's domination and disrespect for
women. Violent sex is a single ingredient recipe for a
relationship? Does it tell a story? Is it to shock? Is it
about culture? Is it revolution? Or is it just about the beat
and clever rhymes? And, of course, big money?

Whatever it is, it seems to appeal to a lot of people - like
the "R" rated (just barely) movies we love to watch. Foul
language, sex, and violence sells.

Still, I wish he would turn it down a little.
I can't hear my own music – which people a generation
before me considered the devil's music. But we believed -
sex, drugs, and rock-n-roll were "groovy" and "that's
where it's at - baby".

Ominous Ambulance

Early in the morning, the hour is small.
Ominous ambulance idles with the headlights on.
Waiting and waiting for that next tragic call?
Have they come for me in the hours before dawn?
Those lights through my window are calling my name.
Is this ride here to whisk me away?
Or someone with injuries or severe chest pain?
Will it be there when night becomes day?
Why is it still there? I need to know.
Making that noise and shining light thru my window.
Then I peek and see two uniforms hiding down low,
Talking and eating relaxed and slow.
And so, I realize it's not me they will take.
It's simply two paramedics on their lunch break.

When Change is Necessary

In order to make important and lasting change-
change that will improve your living conditions and reduce stress-
you must step out of your comfort zone,
face your fears, not make excuses,
make time to do what is necessary,
do not procrastinate,
be strong and not give up,
don't care about what others think,
And don't settle for good enough.

Every Pound Gained

Every pound gained, another notch on the cane.

Another year alone with creaky old bones.

Pain soaks in like hot maple on pancakes.

Weakness puts me on the ground with the grace of an infant.

Time does not heal my ailing joints-

They lay in wait for the next flare up and the next.

But movement, sweet scary movement keeps me from turning to stone.

So I will move, keep on moving - it's what I can do.

Like a Raging River on Fire

Like a raging river on fire, my frustration builds in
intensity and heat.
My mind's eye sees, in blinding darkness, a future that
must be defeated.

Why do I feel so deeply and urgently someone else's pain
and despair?
I work hard to find solutions to problems because I really
care.

Advice given from my heart is sincere and meant for
positive gain.
I don't want to see people I care about suffer emotional
or physical pain.

But when my advice is heard and understood, yet slips
through the fingers,
And the same hurtful disturbing situation lingers,
It makes me confused, a little crazy, and very tired.
All that is left is to cool this fire.

I fear for the future, but it is beyond my control.
There are some things I should not fix or even patrol.
And so, I will ride that river ablaze until it takes me to the
great roaring sea where I can no longer hear the whining
and complaining, and no longer see the torture in their
eyes.

Happy New Year

I sit here shivering on my balcony contemplating a post Christmas silent night.
Colorful lights still chase round and around my neighbor's rooftop tonight.

Christmas tunes are silent now but the songs still echo in my mind.
Torn Christmas wrapping and unraveled bows in bright colors of every kind,
Have been picked up from the curb outside - time to get back to the grind.

I celebrate the hope that the New Year brings.
Hope for health and happiness of family and friends.

Hope for the homeless and sick, that they find their way and be well.
To give back freely of my time and heart to someone in need of help.
Spend time to play and learn, laugh and love, and roar for what's just.

I sit here shivering on my balcony contemplating a snowy midnight celebration.
My mind reviews events of the year - there were times of silent desperation.

But there were also some excellent times of exhilarating inspiration.
It is ice cold in the city but many people eagerly await a

midnight liberation.

I freeze with the rest of the city as I continue my internal narration.

I, finally, raise my glass when I hear fireworks pop and pray for a better year.

A year to appreciate the ones I love and let them know I hold them dear.

Remembering My Mother

She had bright, violet-blue stars in her eyes.
Her laughter was free flowing and contagious.
She was easy to talk to, compassionate and wise.
With her home and her time she was gracious.

Mom could tell jokes as well as any professional.
Her timing was great and she laughed along the way.
Time spent like this was treasured and sensational.
When it was time to go, we all wanted to stay.

She loved mornings spent with coffee and conversation.
In her favorite blue robe she would talk with me for
hours.
For life's problems we would decide on the right solution.
Ideas would flow - you could feel the reason and
brainpower.

She treasured her grandchildren and spoiled them
lovingly.
Mom bought them things that were needed and
cherished.
They loved her for being there for them and listening.
Time spent with her is remembered and relished.

Mom didn't cook - only when she was desperate.
She worshiped chocolate and was often seen in 7-11.
A Marie Calendars fresh peach pie was her favorite.
A Suzie-Q and coffee was her closest thing to heaven.

She spent time each morning applying her lashes and

makeup.

She curled her hair the night before and laid out her clothes for work.
Her morning bath helped her both relax and wakeup.
While doing these things, the coffee began to perk.

I miss her, even now, as the years have passed me by.
Her laughter, her smile I miss more than anything.
I accept that she's gone now, I no longer ask why.
I honor her memory by seeing the lighter side of everything.

About Grieving

Grief makes it hard to breath - hard to fight back tears.

It steals your attention away from what is going on around you.

Everything looses color - all of your senses are dulled.

It is like standing in a small puddle of water,
but feeling like you are drowning in the open sea.

Nothing anyone can say is magic - but being there for hugs and listening is what is needed.

Time, which seems to march on at a funeral processions' pace, does not heal this deep and painful wound completely.

But when a lot of time has passed, the wound will not be as fresh.

You will never be the same, but you will recover your senses and ease back into the world.

Hold tight the loved ones left around you for they may be feeling they have lost you as well.

And know that your loved one, who has passed on, is pulling you through the water so you can make it safely to shore.

I Feel My Pain

Is my tolerance for physical pain low?
How would anyone know that?
Does it really matter?
I feel my pain - no one else can feel it - so how can
anyone determine how well I am tolerating it?
So I should be brave, suck it up, and don't complain?

People recite heroic examples of physical pain they
endured without complaint. That's nice for them. Right?
Be more like so and so who can still manage to walk
around and have conversations while a limb dangles by a
thread- I would call that shock.

It makes them stronger and better human beings if they
can keep from feeling something that should be felt? Or
carrying on as usual with "serious" pain? Are they
showing off and trying to shame me into denial of the
pain I feel? Is it because they can't stand to see me
suffer? This is how they show they care?

I feel my pain and, most times, it hurts. And I embrace it
because it is one thing that I can truly feel and know it is
real.

I feel my pain - no one else can - it's mine.

That's right. I said it. It's my pain. And it hurts. And I
love my pain. Because I can feel it.

The Gas Gage is Pointing to E

The gas gage is pointing to E.
The closest station, five miles away
Let me make it please oh please.

How much is left in mysterious degrees
It went unnoticed how low it was.
The gas gage is pointing to E.

I may have to walk in the pouring freeze.
The needle falls lower and lower.
Let me make it please oh please.

Will I get there? Is such a terrible tease.
I get twenty miles to the gallon.
The gas gage is pointing to E.

To make it would cure my tense unease
And bring relief to the rest of my journey.
Let me make it please oh please.

My nerves are frazzled. I begin to wheeze.
Then I see the sign up the road ahead.
The gas gage is pointing to E.
Let me make it please oh please.

CHAPTER 8 - THE SAFE SIDE

Morning Redundancy

The world turns sunny side up and the morning's
redundancy begins.
Alarm, alarm, alarm, alarm. How many times to hit
snooze again?

Buzzing street lights flicker, then extinguish for the day.
Traffic purrs in all directions along streets and busy
highways.

My neighbor appears in plaid pajamas, yawning and
rubbing his eyes -
While walking his dog, he talks on his phone, and steps
on a sweet surprise.

His screams are heard for miles around, a disturbing
screeching sound-
It awakens the dogs and they start howling, especially,
the angry hounds.

The city bus approaches and stops with a loud, sick
cough.
Passengers pass each other trying to get on and off.

In the shower, I perform an operatic concert or comedic
monologue.
The steam in the bathroom is as thick as a London fog,

So I write a smiley face in the steam on the mirror.
Getting ready for work, coffee helps me think clearer.

I put on my shades, turn my face to the sky, and pray-
that the ones I love, both near and far, have a really
outstanding day.

I am a Wild Bird

I am a restless, wild bird with an enormous wing span,
considerable strength, and stunning beauty.
My feathers are a blend of rich cascading colors-
browns, black, burgundy, and gold.
When I take flight, I rise easily above the noise-
the traffic, sirens, and babies crying.
My shadow moves like a living thing, climbing every
obstacle in its path.
My pride is a pleasing fragrance noticed by many.
I soar faster and higher as my extended wings slice the
frigid air.
Everything on the ground appears smaller,
then disappears in a brown or green blur.
When I plunge swiftly through a canopy of thick white
clouds,
I feel the cold, steamy moisture coat my wings-
It is both cleansing and refreshing.
As I enter that space where white cottony clouds move
with the
roaring wind below;
And above, the brightest rays of the sun warm my back,
I know I am in the best possible place I could be.

How Nature Touches Me

A thunderstorm - a booming symphony of drums played to the flash of lightening cracking the sky. It makes my heart bound with excitement and anticipation.

I love to stand in a cold, gentle rain and feel the moisture slip down my brow and bounce off my eyelashes. It tickles my skin with tiny vibrations as my clothes begin to cling and feel heavy with water.
It is how nature touches me.

I forget everything else and let the rain wash away the grime, the dirt - the negativity.
When the rain and hail pounds the shiny pavement and rooftops, I sit and listen calmed by the unique rhythm it makes.

The air is the freshest and sweetest just after a storm and is a pleasure to breath in.
When a brilliant rainbow stretches across the sky, I feel like I've been given a gift today.

Sunbathing in the Shade

I'm not quite ready to venture out
To seek a relationship; I have my doubts.
Like sunbathing in the shade
With suntan lotion and lemonade.
I'm half way in, half way out
Undecided what to do about
My longing to have a man by my side.
It's been quiet around here where I hide.
But if I wait until I'm ready to start,
I will not learn to risk my heart.
So out of the shade and into the light
I will try to find a love that's just right.

An Executive's Wife

It was a beautiful spring day; perfect tanning weather, I thought. As I ride in my sparkling wine Mercedes convertible blasting my favorite Elvis tape, I take in a deep breath of that tasty diesel perfumed air. Light splashes onto the mirrored windows of my building and I gaze at the distorted image of my car as I drive by.

I pulled into the executive's parking lot and looked for my husband's silver Cadillac Seville - he is the company president, of course. I found his car and pulled up beside it.

Walking into the building, I felt the refreshing swish of cool air from the air-conditioned building. I wanted to walk out and come in again, so I did. The man at the marble security desk inside looked puzzled then laughed at my child-like amusement. I ignored him and headed straight for the elevator, and when the doors were closing, I saw him blow me a kiss. Boy, what beautiful women have to put up with sometimes.

How Good Friends Make Me Feel

Good friends make me feel comfortable; like sitting quietly with a hot cup of coffee and a sweet Danish to greet a brilliant sunrise.

Friends make me feel joyful; like laughing and playing with my cherished pets.

They make me feel cared for, listened to, and understood.

With a friend, I share hopes and dreams, fears and concerns, opinions and advice, and, although some of our beliefs differ, a friend honors and respects those differences. We learn from each other because our eyes see the world in unique ways.

On those miraculous days, when everything goes right - a valued friend makes sure I remember the day as a positive victory.

And when those difficult, challenging days come, and tears are not far beneath the surface, a friend will be there to listen and help me recover.

When I spend time with a valued friend, I can be free to be myself and not be judged.

My soul is warm and blessed because I do have cherished friends that I love.

The Sun Promises

Moving late on a warm Spring afternoon,
I grab my water-bottle, large-brimmed hat, and old
crooked hiking staff. I begin the trek down my favorite
dirt trail and note all the familiar foliage in the colors of
Spring. There is a large, smooth rock off to the side of the
path - I climb to the top. As I sit on this rock and take a
long sip of water, I absorb the view around me. Here
nature reveals its wonders without human interruption. I
hear the play of small birds, lizards running around, and a
light breeze whistling through the canyon. The scenery
and sunlight play a gentle song in my heart. And as I
listen, it entrances me - I become part of the earth on
which I sit. I think of nothing else, and find in myself the
most relaxed state possible. The late afternoon sun
breaths gently on my skin making it warm and glow. And
as the sun disappears beyond a majestic canyon wall, one
last whisper of color sweeps over the valley and I gasp at
its beauty.

Yes, I will return to see the world over again tomorrow-
The sun promises.

The Cold Proud Candle

In the far corner of the living room, beside the window with the white lace curtains drawn; next to a quiet lamp with a shade of pleated linen; there sits a tall red candle standing cold and proud on an antique oak end table, blending in with the night shadows. Supported by a grand brass holder of ornate design, whose luster reflects the dimmest light, the candle's sweet cranberry fragrance is only a faint promise.

But, once its tender wick is ignited, the candle warms and bathes the room with a scent that pleases. The flickering light dances in the air and with shadows on the wall, inspiring relaxation, meditation, and romance. When the candle is extinguished for the night, a whisper of smoke protests and liquid wax hardens - only a taste of the fragrant wax has been burned away. Then the cold, proud candle waits patiently in the dark again – a promise of pleasantry to come.

My Dirty Wailing Wall

When I am frustrated and close to screaming,
I go to my dirty wailing wall and let my mind take me
away for a while-

I fly over the tallest, lush treetops on the wings of a large
raptor; brush over the tips of waves swelling huge in the
ocean; roar in the languages of the fiercest animals on
the planet; reach out and punch a new crater in the face
of the moon; and ride bareback on a graceful horse over
endless, gently rolling meadows.

I envision swaying in a cozy hammock on a spring day
with the newspaper draped over my face and a refreshing
drink not far away.

I ride waterfalls down to fast running rivers that travel far
across the land.

I take my worst angry language and spit it into the
depths of an active volcano.

When I come across a small lake with a mirrored surface,
- I see my reflection and remember who I am and what is
important to me.

And I return to my dirty wailing wall, wipe off the grime
and return to my life - restored.

Boiling Ice Cream

There's a frosty bowl of ice cream in my hand.
His flaming words are painful yet bland.
"I love someone else. Do you understand?"
 I feel ice cream start to melt in my hand.

As I stand there thinking,
my silence is distracting.
My focus is on his prominent nose -
a collision there would be a sweet,
golden send off.
Tapping his feet, poor Babe,
he has urgent business elsewhere.
Stuttering, he screams,
"We're not compatible!"

I have heard enough –
we will no longer embrace.
He needs another woman fluffing his pillowcase.
Then angrily he takes his leave of my place
As boiling ice cream drips from his face.

A Full Moonrise

At moonrise, when the moon is a large and perfect circle,
the longest night shadows are cast.

A mysterious energy fills the air and makes sleep an
impossible task.

I bathe in the light of the cold full moon-
my body swaying as I hum silent and mysterious tunes.

Celebration comes easy like vacationing in Paris;
when the beauty makes me gasp like this.

Through the night, as the moon sweeps across the sky,
every living thing seems animated and energized.

At twilight, when the moon begins to sink behind majestic
mountains, I see "the man on the moon" wink at me at
last– another brilliant, full moon has passed.

A Wondrous Park from My Childhood

In Maryland, where I spent the early years of my childhood, at the end of our street, where the pavement turned into a short dirt road, there was a wondrous park. It was surrounded by a thick wooden fence. The entrance was framed by huge logs on all sides and, when I walked through, it felt like I was entering my own secret world. The first thing you see is a vast field of grass, tall and green in the Spring and Summer; yellow, crunchy, and flattened out in the Fall and Winter. When the grass was green, it grew taller than I was and made me feel hidden and safe. I liked to break off a piece of the stiff green grass and chew on it while I played. Large butterflies and dragonflies of all colors danced around like decorations in the air. There were spaces in the grass for me to lie down and watch white towering cotton ball clouds pass through the bright blue sky above me. Sometimes, I just watched them float around- other times I imagined they were forming particular shapes, animals, or faces.

At the end of the field of grass, there was a dark forest- dark because the trees were so dense and the leaves blocked out most of the sun. No matter how hot it was outside, the forest always seemed cool and the air fresh and sweet. Not far inside the forest, there was a tire swing attached with thick yellow rope to a high sturdy branch. I kicked off my sandals and ran my toes through the cool rich soil. Then jumped into the tire and started swinging. I only noticed the tire's rubber smell for a moment as I swung higher and higher. I loved feeling the breeze brush my face and ripple my clothes; and I loved listening to the loud creaking of the rope on the branch. When I was bored with swinging, I would go deeper into the forest. There were many spider webs around – fully formed ones with intricate designs and geometric shapes. Left undisturbed, spiders can do a lot of art work. Still further, there was a small stream with miniature waterfalls, and more creatures than you can imagine.

Chipmunks ran very fast and frolicked like small children, and would occasionally stop, sit up and stare at you from a safe distance. I never saw anything cuter than a chipmunk - I was never able to catch one. In the water, were eggs from several kinds of critters, tadpoles, tiny fish, tiny snakes, and floating water lilies. On the ground by the stream there were frogs, toads, salamanders, turtles, squirrels, chipmunks, and many types of bugs and beetles. In the trees, there were many Robins and Blue Jays.

I often sat on a large smooth boulder by the stream, listened to the water flow, the sounds of the creatures and birds, and waited for a frog or turtle that I could try to capture.
I loved to go to the park by myself but I would go with friends as well. It was my world, my escape.
I was careful to leave the park before sundown because it got really scary in the absolute darkness, when the owls sat on tree branches, not moving, and watched you with glowing eyes, waiting.

The next morning, I was always happy to return.

Midnight Train

Cast your fears and worries onto a departing midnight train. Leave the past far behind by sending it far away.

Blow tension a kiss through the frosted windows from the platform below. Take your stress and strap it in tight without offering a fluffy pillow.

Imagine train whistles screaming in the face of your despair. Stick your hair pin in the rear of depression and watch it run way out there.

Throw the last of your heavy baggage on that loud out-bound train. No tickets needed, you don't want to go, it's only to take baggage away to relieve emotional pain.

Watch the train disappear in the distance around a bend in the dark. Then breathe in that fresh, newly found freedom and relief in your every part.

It's Coming - Are You Ready

...and the woman exhaled with a deep sigh of release and the sound is a whisper in the lightest winds through a massive canyon - barely heard yet harshly felt. It is coming - am I ready?

...so the woman gathered together her strength and courage to recall, restore, repair, and put away memories of trauma that were barriers to her success and fulfillment, and made fear and anxiety linger.

...and the woman realizes that her history, as agonizing and painful as it was, made her who she is today - a moving tapestry of vivid colors and textures, inked with pain, joy and all in between.

...and the woman re-enters life with a greater understanding of herself and a remarkable letting go. Music sounds sweeter, nature is more vibrant with color and the sounds of birds and small creatures, and flowers are seen as the incredible, beautiful miracles they are.

And so the woman goes forward tall, and brave, determined, clear minded, and free.

Made in the USA
San Bernardino, CA
27 March 2017